Just Saying...

Sayings for Life From a Pastor's Wife

# Janice B. Saulters

Just Saying -Sayings for Life From a Pastor's Wife
Copyright@2022 by Janice B. Saulters
Printed by Kindle Direct Publishing, An Amazon.com Company

Scriptures marked KJV are taken from the KING JAMES VERSION (KJV): KING JAMES VERSION, public domain.

Scriptures taken from the Holy Bible, New International Version®, NIV®. Copyright © 1973, 1978, 1984, 2011 by Biblica, Inc.™ Used by permission of Zondervan. All rights reserved. www.zondervan.com. The "NIV" and "New International Version" are trademarks registered in the United States Patent and Trademark Office by Biblica, Inc.®

ISBN: 979-8-218-03265-4

Library of Congress Control Number: 2022914149

This book was printed in the United States of America

Book Cover Designer: www.ericasmithdesigns.com

# Table of Contents

# Foreword

I met the author, Mrs. Janice Saulters, in 2019. She was a student who came into my office seeking academic assistance and guidance. As I got to know her, I learned of her passion for God and her ministry to spread the Good News of Jesus Christ. I became a published author in 2020 during the pandemic. Janice supported me and my cause by inviting me to her mid-day prayer line. She allowed me to share my testimony of how my relationship with God helped me through my trials and tribulations.

I am honored a phenomenal woman of God asked me to write this foreword for her book. I believe the greatest gift to give is the Word of God. In these writings, you will find just that; words of inspiration and devotionals to support whatever you are going through. God did not promise every day of sunshine, but He did promise His presence and strength to get us through the storms. In this book, Janice has provided His gift. She provides uplifting and encouraging messages to her readers about God and His promises. Janice uses scripture to support her sayings for life from a pastor's wife. God's light shines within her as she relays His message of love through her ministry.

This book will bless you every day during your journey with God. Janice's mantra is to put God first in whatever you do. Job 22:28 (NLT) says, "You will succeed in whatever you choose to do, and light will shine on the road ahead of you." Congratulations Janice! Continue to let your light shine.

Twanice DeLaine Muldrow, Author
"Fire Ice: A Memoir of Love & Pain"
Florence, SC (2022)

# Dedication

There have been so many people who have touched my life and influenced me greatly. This book is a culmination of experiences, along with guidance and godly wisdom I likewise gained along life's journey. First and foremost, I am thankful to my Lord Jesus Christ. Without Him, my purpose and dream of writing a devotional would not have been possible. Next, Pastor Walter Lee and Mother Margaret Jackson have instilled in me a wealth of knowledge and spiritual guidance. To my loving church family and brothers and sisters in Christ, far and near, I thank God for you. Your examples of godly living and invaluable words of encouragement will always be remembered. Blondell Singleton, your helping hands and encouragement have guided me to this momentous landmark.

I cannot forget my "dear" godmother, Gloria Lee, who allowed me to cling to her each Sunday and enjoy doughnuts at her house when I was young. Your influence in my life remains. Aunt Ann, my other "dear one", you have a way with words to move anyone into action, and those words led me to the conclusion of this book project! Last, but certainly not least, I dedicate this devotional in loving memory of my father, Arthur Nathaniel Bluntt, III, who passed away before the completion of this book. Likewise, to my mother, Betty Bluntt, who continues to support and encourage me. Both of you brought me up in the fear and admonition of the Lord. Likewise, Kendall, the nephew who never stops encouraging me to have faith and act!

I am closing this dedication with three people who will always be my heroes--my husband James, along with our two children, Bradley and Sidnee. You all are my greatest motivators. Our struggles, our dreams, our hopes, and our triumphs are the reasons why this book is a reality today. Thank you.

# Introduction

Have you ever dreamed or desired to do something great for the Kingdom of God? Have you ever wondered how you can accomplish something that seems like something only great people accomplish? Philippians 4:13 is a perfect reminder of what you can do to fulfill your purpose in life. It states: "I can do all things through Christ which strengtheneth me." This devotional was born out of the belief that you don't have to be great to achieve the task of writing a book or any task, for that matter. However, I *am* in Christ, so I am already great!

The words in this devotional are truly God-inspired. Some words are born out of personal experiences and testimonies, while others simply depict the script of everyday living. They remind us of the presence of the Holy Spirit that is alive, at work, and flowing like a well of living water in the lives of believers.

Likewise, the quotes and poems highlighted in this timely devotional reflect the symbol of the leaf. In many cultures around the world, leaves generally symbolize fertility and growth. Green leaves, in particular, represent hope, renewal, and revival. In other cultures, leaves symbolize hope amid difficulties and hardships. Thus, every God-breathed word in this book will radiate the hope of God's promises and remind you of new life and hope that only He can give. Therefore, be endowed, encouraged, and enriched as you read God's words and obey His calling in your life!

# Inspirational Quotes

This heartfelt devotional is drenched in empowering quotes and God-breathed Scriptures.

Come journey with Janice Saulters and sit at the feet of Jesus. You will receive enlightenment and become more resilient in your walk with the Lord.

*You* write the vision. I'll make the provision. -God

And the Lord answered me, and said, Write the vision, and make it plain upon tables, that he may run that readeth it.

For the vision is yet for an appointed time, but at the end it shall speak, and not lie: though it tarry, wait for it; because it will surely come, it will not tarry.

-Habakkuk 2:2

## Hurt in order to heal.

The Lord is nigh unto them that are of a broken heart; and saveth such as be of a contrite spirit.

Many are the afflictions of the righteous: but the Lord delivereth him out of them all.

-Psalms 34:18-19

Come unto me, all ye that labour and are heavy laden, and I will give you rest.

-Matthew 11:28

# If you can't laugh, why live?

A merry heart doeth good like a medicine: but a broken spirit drieth the bones.

-Proverbs 17:22

All the days of the afflicted are evil: but he that is of a merry heart hath a continual feast.

-Proverbs 15:15

# The world says you can't, but God says you can.

I can do all things through Christ which strengtheneth me.

-Philippians 4:13

Fear thou not; for I am with thee: be not dismayed; for I am thy God: I will strengthen thee; yea, I will help thee; yea, I will uphold thee with the right hand of my righteousness.

-Isaiah 41:10

*The* words of a song bring meaning to life.  The melody brings joy to the soul.

Speaking to yourselves in psalms and hymns and spiritual songs, singing and making melody in your heart to the Lord.

-Ephesians 5:19

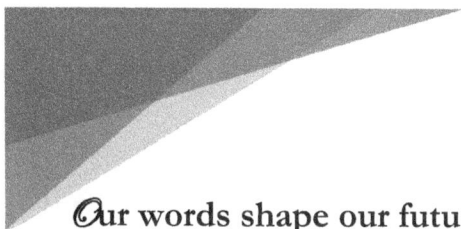

**Our words shape our future.**

**Our life tells our story.**

Death and life are in the power of the tongue: and they that love it shall eat the fruit thereof.

-Proverbs 18:21

## Time takes its course and leads us to the inevitable things in life.

Whereas ye know not what shall be on the morrow. For what is your life: It is even a vapour, that appeareth for a little time, and then vanisheth away.

-James 4:14

*Some things are possible by reason or by default, but all things are possible through faith in God.*

And Jesus answering saith unto them, Have faith in God. For verily I say unto you, that whosoever shall say unto this mountain, be thou removed, and be thou cast into the sea; and shall not doubt in his heart, but shall believe that those things which he saith shall come to pass; he shall have whatsoever he saith.

Therefore I say unto you, What things soever ye desire, when ye pray, believe that ye receive them, and ye shall have them.

-Mark 11:23-24

**Greatness comes in small doses of faith.**

And Jesus said unto them, Because of your unbelief: for verily I say unto you, If you have faith as a grain of mustard seed, ye shall say unto this mountain, remove hence to yonder place; and it shall remove; and nothing shall be impossible unto you.

-Matthew 17:20

And Jesus answering saith unto them, Have faith in God.

-Mark 11:22

*You* don't have to be great in order to shine.

Ye are the light of the world. A city that is set on an hill cannot be hid.

Neither do men light a candle, and put it under a bushel, but on a candlestick; and it giveth light unto all that are in the house.

Let your light so shine before men, that they may see your good works, and glorify your Father which is in heaven.

-Matthew 5:14-16

## Strength comes from growing and growing comes from strength.

The Lord is my light and my salvation; whom shall I fear? The Lord is the strength of my life; of whom shall I be afraid.

-Psalms 27:1

The Lord is my strength and song, and he is become my salvation: he is my God, and I will prepare him a habitation; my father's God, and I will exalt him.

-Exodus 15:2

## Little is more in the kingdom of God.

Another parable put he forth unto them, saying, The kingdom of heaven is like to a grain of mustard seed, which a man took, and sowed in his field:

Which indeed is the least of all seeds: but when it is grown, it is the greatest among herbs, and becometh a tree, so that the birds of the air come and lodge in the branches thereof.

-Matthew 13:31-32

## Happiness is earned through obedience.

Blessed are the undefiled in the way, who walk in the law of the Lord.

Blessed are they that keep his testimonies, and that seek him with the whole heart.

-Psalms 119:1-2

Blessed is every one that feareth the Lord; that walketh in his ways.

For thou shalt eat the labour of thine hands: happy shalt thou be, and it shall be well with thee.

-Psalms 128:1-2

## Human promises tend to fail while God's promises always prevail.

It is better to trust in the Lord than to put confidence in man.

It is better to trust in the Lord than to put confidence in princes.

-Psalms 118:8-9

The Lord is not slack concerning his promise, as some men count slackness; but is longsuffering to us-ward, not willing that any should perish, but that all should come to repentance.

-2 Peter 3:9

## (Choices) We choose, but the outcomes rule!

Be not deceived; God is not mocked: for whatsoever a man soweth, that shall he also reap.

For he that soweth to his flesh shall of the flesh reap corruption; but he that soweth to the Spirit shall of the Spirit reap life everlasting.

-Galatians 6:7-8

**Time wasted is faith without action.**

Even so faith, if it hath not works, is dead being alone.

Yea, a man may say, Thou has faith, and I have works: show me thy faith without thy works, and I will show thee my faith by my works.

- James 2:17-18

# *I* can live for today but tomorrow is not promised.

Go to now, ye that say, To day or to morrow we will go into such a city, and continue there a year, and buy and sell, and get gain:

Whereas ye know not what shall be on the morrow. For what is your life? It is even a vapour, that appeareth for a little time, and then vanisheth away.

For that ye ought to say, If the Lord will, we shall live, and do this, or that.

-James 4:13-15

Boast not thyself of to morrow; for thou knowest not what a day may bring forth.

-Proverbs 27:1

*Following* has choices. Leading has challenges. Don't be afraid to lead.

And the LORD shall make thee the head and not the tail; and thou shalt be above only, and thou shalt not be beneath; if that thou hearken unto the commandments of the LORD thy God, which I command thee this day, to observe and to do them:

-Deuteronomy 28:13

*L*isten to your heart if your heart is following God.

Keep thy heart with all diligence; for out of it are the issues of life.

-Proverbs 4:23

Trust in the Lord with all thine heart; and lean not unto thine own understanding. In all thy ways acknowledge him, and he shall direct thy paths.

-Proverbs 3:5-6

Then Nathan said unto David, Do all that is in thine heart; for God is with thee.

-1 Chronicles 17:2

## The keys of God's kingdom only work when used.

And I will give unto thee the keys of the kingdom of heaven: and whatsoever thou shalt bind on earth shall be bound in heaven: and whatsoever thou shalt loose on earth shall be loosed in heaven.

-Matthew 16:19

**Spend your life on things that will last; not a fortune on things that will perish.**

If ye then be risen with Christ, seek those things which are above, where Christ sitteth on the right hand of God.

Set your affection on things above, not on things on the earth

For ye are dead, and your life is hid with Christ in God.

When Christ, *who is* our life, shall appear, then shall ye also appear with him in glory.

- Colossians 3:1-4

## Opportunity is always knocking. When will you answer?

Behold, I stand at the door and knock: if any man hear my voice, and open the door, I will come into him, and will sup with him, and he with me.

-Revelation 3:20

**When Jesus knocks, open your heart and let Him in.**

While it is said, To day if ye will hear his voice, harden not your hearts, as in the provocation.

-Hebrews 3:15

## Faith requires obedience, and obedience requires faith.

But without faith it is impossible to please him: for he that cometh to God must believe that he is, and that he is a rewarder of them that diligently seek him.

-Hebrews 11:6

By faith Abraham, when he was called to go out into a place which he should after receive for an inheritance, obeyed; and he went out, not knowing whither he went.

-Hebrews 11:8

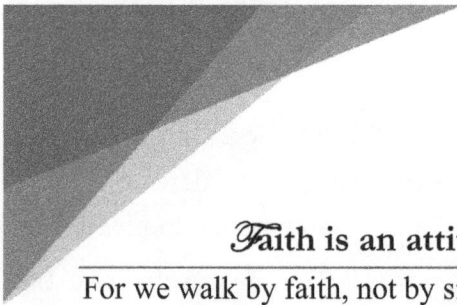

## Faith is an attitude!

For we walk by faith, not by sight.

- 2 Corinthians 5:7

But without faith it is impossible to please him: for he that cometh to God must believe that he is, and that he is a rewarder of them that diligently seek him.

-Hebrews 11:6

## Change your thinking and the outcomes change.

For as he thinketh in his heart, so is he.

-Proverbs 23:7(a)

## Faith moves us forward. Doubt sets us back.

Even so faith, if it hath not works,
is dead, being alone.

-James 2:17

**Cry if you must; just don't drown in your tears.**

The righteous cry, and the LORD heareth, and delivereth them out of all their troubles.

-Psalms 34:16

## God's will be done. I insist.

Thy kingdom come, Thy will be
done in earth, as it is in heaven.

-Matthew 6:10

## Yesterday is gone. I am moving on.

Remember ye not the former things, neither consider the things of old.           -Isaiah 43:18

Brethren, I count not myself to have apprehended: but this one thing I do, forgetting those things which are behind, and reaching forth unto those things which are before.

-Philippians 3:13

**Change is inevitable because nothing remains the same except God and His Word!**

The grass withereth, the flower fadeth: but the word our God shall stand forever.

-Isaiah 40:8

## Life without laughter is lonely.

All the days of the afflicted are evil: but he that is of a merry heart hath a continual feast.

-Proverbs 15:15

## I am destined, determined, and divinely appointed.

For I know the thoughts that I think toward you, saith the Lord, thoughts of peace, and not of evil, to give you an expected end.

-Jeremiah 29:11

*If* you think you can't, you won't. If you believe you can, you will.

I can do all things through Christ which strengtheneth me.

-Philippians 4:13

## Prayer is my sanity.

But thou, when thou prayest, enter into thy closet, and when thou hast shut thy door, pray to thy Father which is in secret; and thy Father which seeth in secret shall reward thee openly.

-Matthew 6:6

Pray without ceasing.

-1 Thessalonians 5:17

Likewise, the Spirit also helpeth our infirmities: for we know not what we should pray for as we ought: but the Spirit itself maketh intercession for us with groanings which cannot be uttered.

-Romans 8:26

*L*ve for today.  God will take care of tomorrow.

But seek ye first the kingdom of God and his righteousness, and all these things shall be added unto you.

Take therefore no thought for the morrow: for the morrow shall take thought for the things of itself. Sufficient unto the day is the evil thereof.

-Matthew 6:33-34

## Nothing surprises God.

Great is our Lord, and of great power: his understanding is infinite.

-Psalms 147:5

Before I formed thee in the belly I knew thee; and before thou camest forth out of the womb I sanctified thee, and I ordained thee a prophet unto the nations.

-Jeremiah 1:5

Can any hide himself in secret places that I shall not see him? saith the LORD. Do not I fill heaven and earth? saith the LORD."

-Jeremiah 23:24

For he looketh to the ends of the earth, and seeth under the whole heaven; To make the weight for the winds; and he weigheth the waters by measure.

-Job 28:24-25

## God—the answer to life

Jesus saith unto him, I am the way, the truth, and the life no man cometh unto the Father, but by me.

-John 14:6

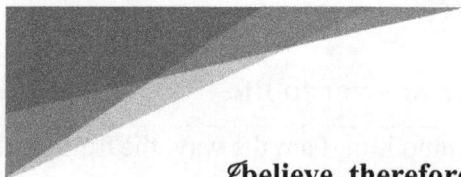

## *I* believe, therefore, I am.

For God hath not given us the spirit of fear; but of power, and of love, and of a sound mind.

-2 Timothy 1:7

# *Overflow*

## An overflow of God-inspired quotes

The words of the mouth are deep waters, but the fountain of wisdom is a rushing stream.

-Proverbs 18:4, NIV

You cannot live for yesterday because it's already gone. Live for today and move on.

When you imagine, you dream.

When you believe, you achieve.

Don't let troubles surprise you. They are sure to come.

We are all in a race.

Run to the end.

When life gets busy,
don't crowd God out.

The simple goes unnoticed, but makes an impact in the kingdom of God.

Live in order to give
because living is giving.

Time and change will happen;
it's just a matter of time.

Take nothing for granted; for all that is granted is given by God.

Wishing only hinders progress.

When it hurts, it hurts.

Live like you are going somewhere
eternally.

Nothing happens beyond God's timing.

Run, walk, skip, or slide—we all have a race to finish.

Life is like a race—there is a starting point and a finish line.

Because of whose I am, I know who I am.

The end is only as far away as you think.

Can't only exists when doubt
shows up.

God's plan always works.

Pray. Believe. Repeat.

Pray before you do anything because anything is possible when you pray.

I am as strong as my faith is in God.

Anxiety produces fear, but faith produces patience.

The most precious treasures
are hidden in God's Word.

I believe God because I know
He will.

My agenda, but God's plan prevails.

Laughter brings life to the soul.

Today is already a good day. Make it great with the choices you make.

Let love dominate so hatred will dissipate.

Mistakes happen and may cause you to fall; but learn from the mistakes and always try again.

You don't win simply by reason of strength. It comes through the determination you have within.

Take all the time you want,
but time will not wait on you.

I am not living for an earthly prize because Heaven is my reward.

Shine every day because your life is always on display.

Treat others with the utmost respect because you deserve nothing less.

Living godly only costs
your life.

Life beginning is the beginning of life. Take your time and live.

Your attitude is your life.

Stop blaming others when you can blame yourself.

Don't wait for others to praise you. That may never happen.

Reach your goals before
you reach the limit.

Nothing can stop
determination.

You will go far if you
don't keep looking back.

If you can worry, then you can pray; and when you have doubt, replace it with faith.

You might have to go through,
but you will get there.

# *Poetry*

Oh that my words were now written! oh that they were printed in a book!

That they were graven with an iron pen and lead in the rock for ever!

-Job 19:23-24

# You Are Not Hopeless

Struggle if you must. Cry when there is distrust. But you are not hopeless.

You are weary when you are tired; afraid when you go through the fire. But hold on, be strong, for you are not hopeless.

When your strength is failing and your eyes are getting dim, that's the time to trust *Him* because you are not hopeless.

When problems stack high, you feel God is not nigh, draw strength from the spirit within. You are not hopeless.

Options in life may be simple and few. Look to God who will lead you. He knows what to do.

The answers may not seem certain. Your end may be near. Hope and trust to the end, you are not hopeless.

# Who Will Stand Up?

Wars, troubles, inflation, abuse;
Turmoil, heartaches, and confusion too.
Mistrust, hatred, anguish, and pain;
Deception, destruction, and death
All for the sake of personal gain.
Who will stand up and blaze a path that is made
plain?

The poor, the hungry, and the homeless cry out,
While people stand up and look aimlessly about.
Broken hearts and hurting souls.
Who will help ease their pain?
Who will come to their rescue?
Who will give a helping hand?
Who I ask will simply take a stand?

The reality of life seems all too familiar.
Lives are taken and crime is on the rise.
Just who will stand up and heed; to the feigning
cries?

While nothing is certain except God's Word alone,
Who will stand up and proclaim that He is still on
the throne?
Watching and waiting for souls to heed
The call and promise of salvation on bended knees.

Who will stand up and compel men to come?
Who will stand up for this race is not done?

# Yes Lord

Yes Lord, here I am.
I am here to serve you.
Yes Lord, yes Lord, do what you please to do.

My mouth, my hands, my feet are yours.
I want to serve you and you alone.
Teach me, lead me, guide me into paths for you.
Yes Lord, yes Lord, do what you please to do.

I am weak, I am frail, and my life is but a vapor.
But each day I live, your mercies are new.
Do with my life what you please to do.

The heart gets heavy and burdens surmount.
But I will bear the cross with the strength that you allow.
Yes, Lord, I am here to serve you.
Do with my life what you please to do.

I am bought with a price.
I am no longer my own.
You made me brand new.
Do with my life what you please to do.

Yes Lord, here I am.
I am here to serve you.
Yes Lord, yes Lord, do what you please to do.

# Secret Place

Beat down, torn, broken, battered;
Abused, sad, hurt, and tattered.

Stay there, cry there, what is left to do?
Lay there, pray there, will you come through?

Secret place and all alone;
Quiet, dark, an agonizing moan.

Blurt out, cry out, but the words make no sense.
Weary, worn, and nothing left to give.

Small voice, inner peace, warm touch of love;
Nothing to see, nothing to touch except the
Presence of the Father above.

# Give God Your All

Mediocrity and slothfulness work hand in hand;
No rush, no goal, no sight, no plan.

Whenever, wherever, that's how it goes.
Wasted time, wasted efforts, that's how your life
flows.

Preoccupied with senseless thoughts,
When battles for souls are waiting to be fought.

Reality and truth are knocking at your heart's
door; give up, yield, and yearn for more.

There is life to live.
There is life to give.

Answer the call.
Give God your all.

# Meet the Author

Janice B. Saulters is a native of Charleston, South Carolina where she grew up on James Island and completed elementary, middle, and high school. She also attended Converse College and later completed a degree in leadership and management. She currently resides in Summerville, South Carolina with her family. Janice has been married to her husband, James, for 28 years and they have two children, Bradley and Sidnee. Janice grew up in church all of her life and she holds a special place in her heart for older saints of God.

She cherishes the memories of growing up and spending hours and days in the presence of godly, spirit-filled women. Their influence and godly wisdom have helped mold and shape her into the woman of God and Kingdom ambassador she is today. When Janice is not writing, teaching music, or working with youth and young adults in her church and community, she is doing what she is very passionate about—playing the violin. She volunteers and plays at the community hospital and senior facilities. Janice takes pride and displays much joy when she is working for the Lord and utilizing her gifts for the Kingdom of God!

# Resource Guide

1. <u>Leaves Twig Watercolor - Free image on Pixabay</u>

# AVAILABLE NOW -AMAZON

# PONDER

# PONDER

# PONDER

*9 7 9 8 2 1 8 0 3 2 6 5 4 *